THE BUCKEYE STATE

by Michael A. Martin

Curriculum Consultant: Jean Craven,
Director of Instructional Support,
Albuquerque, NM, Public Schools

WORLD ALMANAC® LIBRARY

Please visit our web site at: www.worldalmanaclibrary.com
For a free color catalog describing World Almanac® Library's list of high-quality books
and multimedia programs, call 1-800-848-2928 or fax your request to (414) 332-3567.

Library of Congress Cataloging-in-Publication Data

Martin, Michael A.
    Ohio, the Buckeye State / by Michael A. Martin.
      p. cm. — (World Almanac Library of the states)
    Includes bibliographical references and index.
    Summary: Illustrations and text present the history, geography, people, politics and
government, economy, and social life and customs of Ohio.
    ISBN 0-8368-5124-2 (lib. bdg.)
    ISBN 0-8368-5290-7 (softcover)
    1. Ohio—Juvenile literature. [1. Ohio.] I. Title. II. Series.
F491.3.M37   2002
977.1—dc21   2001046994

This edition first published in 2002 by
World Almanac® Library
330 West Olive Street, Suite 100
Milwaukee, WI 53212 USA

This edition © 2002 by World Almanac® Library.

Design and Editorial: **Jack&Bill**/Bill SMITH STUDIO Inc.
Editors: Jackie Ball and Kristen Behrens
Art Directors: Ron Leighton and Jeffrey Rutzky
Photo Research and Buying: Christie Silver and Sean Livingstone
Design and Production: Maureen O'Connor and Jeffrey Rutzky
World Almanac® Library Editors: Patricia Lantier, Amy Stone, Valerie J. Weber,
Catherine Gardner, Carolyn Kott Washburne, Alan Wachtel, Monica Rausch
World Almanac® Library Production: Scott M. Krall, Eva Erato-Rudek, Tammy Gruenewald

Photo credits: p. 5 © PhotoDisc; p. 6 (bottom left) © Corel, (bottom right) © Corel, (top right)
© Corel; p. 7 (top) © PhotoDisc, (bottom) © ArtToday; p. 9 © PhotoDisc; p. 10 © Lee
Snider/CORBIS; p. 11 © ArtToday; p. 12 © PhotoDisc; p. 13 © ArtToday; p. 14 (all) © Library of
Congress; p. 15 © Wolfgang Kaehler/CORBIS; p. 17 © Steve Liss/TimePix; p. 18 © PhotoDisc;
p. 19 © Steve Liss/TimePix; p. 20 (from left to right) © Painet, © Painet, © Marcia Schonberg,
© PhotoDisc, © Louie Anderson, Akron CVB; p. 23 © Corel; p. 26 (all) © PhotoDisc; p. 29
© Lee Snider/CORBIS; p. 30 © Library of Congress; p. 31 (all) © Library of Congress; p. 32
© PhotoDisc; p. 33 (top) © Joan Tiefel, (bottom) © Roger Mastroianni; p. 34 (top) © Library of
Congress, (bottom) © Joan Tiefel; p. 35 © ArtToday; p. 36 © Corel; p. 37 courtesy of Cleveland
CVB; p. 39 (top) © PhotoDisc, (bottom) © Dover Publications; p. 40 (top left) © Library of
Congress, (bottom left) © George Shelton/NASA/TimePix, (bottom right) © John
Olsen/TimePix; p. 41 (top) NASA; p. 42 © Library of Congress; p. 44 (all) © PhotoDisc; p. 45
(top) © ArtToday, (bottom) © Carl Mydans/TimePix

Printed in the United States of America

1 2 3 4 5 6 7 8 9 06 05 04 03 02

Ohio

All Things Possible

The story of Ohio is a tale of centuries of change, sometimes slow and steady, other times abrupt and wrenching. Once the homeland of native peoples whose large-scale engineering projects still stand today, Ohio later became a jumping-off place into regions of North America never before seen by people of European descent. Today Ohio is an integral part of our nation's midwestern heartland. Ohio's cities are known for art, culture, commerce, and industry, urban centers set against the backdrop of Ohio's natural beauty.

Shaped like a waving U.S. flag, Ohio stands astride four very different geographical regions of North America: the Great Lakes Plains (specifically Lake Erie) to the northeast; the agriculturally rich western Till Plains (part of North America's interior lowlands); the mineralogical treasure trove of the eastern Appalachian (or Allegheny) Plateau; and the forested, southwestern Bluegrass Region. Among the state's other prominent natural features are the numerous twists and turns of the Ohio River, whose name derives from an Iroquois word meaning "great water." The river, in turn, gives the state of Ohio its name.

Covering an area of 40,948 square miles (106,055 square kilometers), Ohio ranks only thirty-fifth in geographical size. Ohio's population is relatively large, however — the seventh largest of any U.S. state.

Ohio, whose people represent cultures from all over the world, has produced many important citizens whose imprints upon history are indelible. Among these are seven U.S. presidents and renowned authors, artists, and inventors. Ohioans Wilbur and Orville Wright created the airplane; Thomas Edison invented the electric light; and Neil Armstrong, the first human being to walk on the surface of the Moon, hailed from Ohio. Ohioans have played a major role in shaping U.S. history.

▶ Map of Ohio, showing interstate highway system, as well as major cities and waterways.

▼ A misty morning in Ohio.

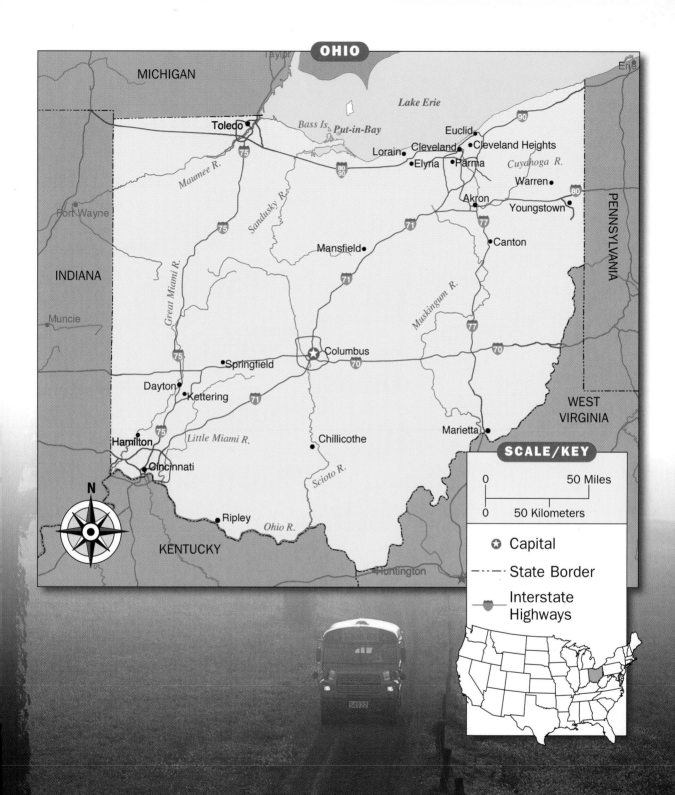

OHIO

MICHIGAN

Taylor

Lake Erie

Bass Is.
Put-in-Bay

Toledo

Maumee R.

Sandusky R.

Euclid
Cleveland • Cleveland Heights
Lorain • Parma
Elyria
Cuyahoga R.
Warren

Fort Wayne

INDIANA

Great Miami R.

Mansfield

Akron
Youngstown

Canton

Muskingum R.

Muncie

Springfield
Columbus

Dayton
Kettering

Little Miami R.

Hamilton

Chillicothe

Marietta

Cincinnati

Scioto R.

N

Ripley
Ohio R.

KENTUCKY

Huntington

PENNSYLVANIA

WEST
VIRGINIA

SCALE/KEY

0   50 Miles

0   50 Kilometers

⭐ Capital

—··— State Border

Interstate
Highways

Fast Facts

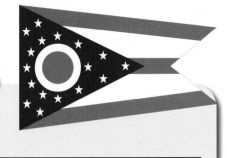

OHIO (OH), The Buckeye State

Entered Union

March 1, 1803 (17th state)

Capital	Population
Columbus	711,470

Total Population (2000)

11,353,140 (7th most populous state)

Largest Cities	Population
Columbus	711,470
Cleveland	478,403
Cincinnati	331,285
Toledo	313,619

Land Area

40,948 square miles (106,055 square kilometers) (35th largest state)

State Motto

"With God, All Things Are Possible."

State Song

"Beautiful Ohio," *words by Ballard MacDonald and music by Mary Earl.*

State Animal

White-tailed deer

State Bird

Cardinal

State Fish

Walleye

State Insect

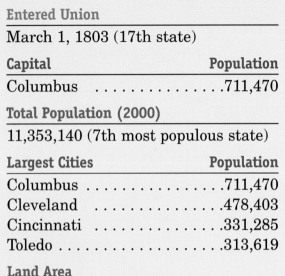

Ladybug — *Also known as ladybird beetles, ladybugs feed on many species of harmful insect pests.*

State Tree

Ohio buckeye — *This tree's nut was known to Indians as* hetuck, *or "eye of the buck." Ohioans later came to call it the Ohio buckeye, or "stinking buckeye," because its flowers and wood have an unpleasant smell.*

State Flower

Scarlet carnation — *Ohio adopted the scarlet carnation as its state flower in memory of slain U.S. president William McKinley, an Ohioan who often wore this flower in his lapel.*

State Wildflower

White trillium

State Reptile

Black racer snake — *Known as the "farmer's friend" because it eats disease-carrying rodents, the black racer snake became Ohio's official state reptile in 1995, after legislators received a persuasive letter from a young boy named Jacob Mercer.*

State Beverage

Tomato juice — *Ohio is the nation's leading tomato juice producer. Only California produces more tomatoes than Ohio.*

PLACES TO VISIT

Rutherford B. Hayes Library and Museum, *Fremont*
Located at the former U.S. president's Spiegel Grove estate, the library houses the papers of Rutherford Birchard Hayes as well as books on nineteenth-century U.S. life. Open since 1916, this was the nation's first presidential library.

Rock and Roll Hall of Fame and Museum, *Cleveland*
This interactive museum not only enshrines the accomplishments and artifacts of rock-and-roll's most influential recording artists, it also maintains a busy schedule of public events, including lectures and concerts.

The Rankin House, *Ripley*
The home of Presbyterian minister John Rankin was an important stop on the Underground Railroad. Between 1825 and 1865 more than two thousand escaped slaves passed through this house on their way to freedom in Canada.

For other places and events to attend, see p. 44

BIGGEST, BEST, AND MOST

- World's tallest steel-track roller coaster.
- World leader in the production of machine tools, and clay and rubber products.
- World's biggest soup factory.
- World's leading producer of frozen pizzas.

STATE FIRSTS

- 1869 — Cleveland Abbe, the director of the Cincinnati Observatory, released the first public weather forecast on September 1 of that year.
- 1967 — The city of Cleveland elected as its mayor Carl B. Stokes, the first African American to hold this post in a major U.S. city.

Matchless

Philadelphia lawyer Joshua Pusey invented the first book of matches. Diamond Brands got the patent from Pusey, and the first book of matches was produced, in 1896, in Barberton. The date of the original patent, September 27, 1892, appeared on Diamond matchbooks for many years thereafter. In 1942 Diamond Brands developed a match that could be soaked in water for up to eight hours and still light.

In Memory of Martha

On September 1, 1914, Martha, the last known American passenger pigeon, a bird native to North America, died in captivity in the Cincinnati Zoo. Until the mid-1800s there had been more passenger pigeons than any other bird in the world, but the birds were hunted for their meat and, as of the 1890s, had completely disappeared from the wild. The passenger pigeon was the first native American animal to become extinct. The Passenger Pigeon Memorial, originally an aviary where Martha lived, still stands in the Cincinnati Zoo and is today a National Historic Landmark.

Ancient but Everchanging Frontier

> A country beautiful and fertile, and affording . . . all that nature had decreed for the comfort of man.
>
> — *Morris Birkbeck (an English traveler in Ohio), 1817*

The First Ohioans

By at least seven thousand years ago, the Ohio region had become home to a succession of native peoples who made the most of the natural abundance left behind by retreating Ice Age glaciers (large, slow-moving bodies of ice). Ohio's earliest residents probably came in pursuit of game animals, such as mastodon and giant beaver. These hunters were soon replaced by more advanced native peoples, groups now collectively known as mound builders because of their practice of constructing large religious monuments out of earth. The mound builders left behind more than six thousand burial and ceremonial mounds, forts, and other earthen structures throughout Ohio, as well as in other states and in Canada; many of their works still exist today.

The three principal Ohio mound-building peoples were the Adena (who began creating monuments in about 700 B.C.), the Hopewell (who flourished between about 600 B.C. and A.D. 500), and the Mississippians (who lasted from about A.D. 700 until the 1700s). By the time Europeans began to explore and settle the Ohio region, the native peoples they encountered included such groups as the Erie, Wyandot (or Huron), Ottawa, and Tuscarora, who lived in the north; the Delaware and Shawnee, who occupied the south; the Iroquois League (or Mingo) to the east; and the western-dwelling Miami people.

European Exploration

No one knows for certain which European first set foot in Ohio country, but this honor goes either to Rene-Robert Cavelier, Sieur de La Salle, or to Louis Jolliet, both natives of France. La Salle journeyed through the Ohio River region

Native Americans of Ohio
Delaware
Erie
Iroquois
Miami
Ottawa
Shawnee
Tuscarora
Wyandot, also known as Huron

Ancient Native American Cultures
Adena (between about 700 B.C. and A.D. 100)
Hopewell (between about 600 B.C. and A.D. 500)
Mississippian (between about A.D. 700 until the 1700s)

between 1669 and 1670, while Jolliet explored Lake Erie. In 1750 the Ohio Company of Virginia (a private firm) dispatched Christopher Gist to explore the upper Ohio River Valley. This company, organized in 1747, was made up of Englishmen and Virginians who planned to build settlements in the Ohio region. In 1761 the French laid claim to the entire Ohio Valley, based upon the maps and explorations of La Salle. The British, however, claimed all the territory extending inland from their Atlantic colonies. Although the French had never had any permanent settlements in the Ohio Territory, they struggled bitterly against the English for control of the region.

War and Rebellion

Territorial disputes between England and France led to the French and Indian War (1754–1763). The war concluded with England acquiring most of the former French territory east of the Mississippi River, including the disputed Ohio

▼ Rolling hills in Ohio farmland.

region. Shortly after the signing of the 1763 treaty that ended the war, an Ohio-born Indian chief named Pontiac began an Indian uprising against the British, an effort that ultimately failed.

Nearly a decade later the British were once again at war — this time with their own thirteen North American colonies — in a conflict known as the Revolutionary War (1775–1783). Although the Ohio Territory was not one of the thirteen rebellious colonies, the Revolutionary War had a definite effect on the Ohio region. In 1776 the fighting spilled into Ohio, causing the abandonment of a Moravian mission settlement called Schoenbrunn, which had been founded in 1772 near present-day New Philadelphia. In 1780 George Rogers Clark won the Battle of Piqua (near present-day Springfield), defeating England's Shawnee allies and scoring an important victory. After the war the Ohio country became a possession of the newly independent United States.

The Ohio Territory and a Clash of Cultures

The Ohio country became part of the Northwest Territory after the passage of the Ordinances of 1785 and 1787. These measures instituted a stable government in the territory. They also encouraged land surveying and sales, causing

▼ In the eighteenth century Moravians in Ohio lived in log cabins like this one at the reconstructed Shoenbrunn Village.

settlement by Anglo-Americans to accelerate. In addition they laid the groundwork for Ohio's eventual statehood. The states of Connecticut and Virginia maintained ownership of the Ohio Territory, dividing it up as the Connecticut Western Reserve in the northeast and the Virginia Military District in the southwest (between the Little Miami and Scioto Rivers). In 1787 the private Ohio Company of Associates also acquired some land in Ohio — 1,875 square miles (4,856 square kilometers) of it — and established Marietta, Ohio's very first town, in 1788. Later that year Cincinnati was founded near the Ohio River.

European settlers came into frequent conflict with the native peoples of Ohio, who responded by initiating raids and uprisings. Several of these raids were led by a Miami chief named Little Turtle, and the British government also had a hand in fomenting native unrest.

In 1794 the remnants of the Erie, Huron, Ottawa, Tuscarora, Iroquois, Delaware, Miami, and Shawnee tribes became embroiled in battle against the U.S. Army. Under the leadership of the Shawnee chief Blue Jacket, this Native-American fighting force met its defeat in the Battle of Fallen Timbers at the hands of General Anthony ("Mad Anthony") Wayne. This battle led to the establishment the following year of the Greenville Treaty Line, which separated the northwest Native-American lands from the regions in the east and south; these lands were set aside for U.S. settlement.

The treaty gave the United States about two-thirds of what is now Ohio, and the Native peoples accepted it largely because of the persuasion of a Wyandot chief named Crane (also known as Tarhe). During the next several decades, the pace of pioneer settlement accelerated further, forcing the native peoples from their remaining lands tribe by tribe. In 1842 the last remaining tribal lands in Ohio were ceded to the United States by the Wyandot.

Pontiac's War

A chief of the Ottawa tribe, Pontiac (born around 1720 in northern Ohio, near Detroit, MI) was a significant Native-American leader of the eighteenth century. Trying to keep the Great Lakes and the Ohio and Mississippi valleys under Indian control, Pontiac tried to unite all the native peoples of these regions. After the French and Indian War broke out (1754–1763), Pontiac led his people in an alliance with the French against the British, although he rejected the territorial claims of both powers. After receiving pledges of military assistance from the French, Pontiac captured nine British forts in 1763. This initiative, known as Pontiac's War, ultimately failed because the promised French aid never came. Pontiac later became a priest of the Midewiwin (Grand Medicine) Society and was assassinated by a Peoria Indian at Cahokia, Illinois, on April 20, 1769.

The city of Columbus stands on the edge of the Scioto River.

The British Are Coming — Again!

Ohioans played an active role in defending the young United States from British attacks during the War of 1812 (1812–1815). On September 10, 1813, Commodore Oliver H. Perry defeated a British fleet at the Battle of Lake Erie. Perry's Victory and International Peace Memorial now stands on South Bass Island at Lake Erie's Put-in-Bay. The monument commemorates Perry's naval achievement as well as almost two centuries of peace between the United States and Canada. The memorial is one of the nation's tallest, with a granite shaft towering 352 feet (107 m) high. It is outfitted with an observation deck at its summit.

Statehood

In 1800 the United States Congress passed the Division Act to divide up the large area known as the Northwest Territory. The western section became known as Indian Territory. Within Indian Territory, a smaller area was designated Ohio Territory, with its capital at Chillicothe. When a 1797 census counted more than five thousand adult (white) males in the Ohio region, it became clear that statehood lay in the near future. A convention met in November, 1802, in Chillicothe to draft a state constitution. On March 1, 1803, Ohio became the seventeenth state to enter the Union, with Edward Tiffin serving as the new state's first governor. Chillicothe was Ohio's state capital until 1810, when it was briefly replaced by Zanesville. In

1812 Chillicothe once again became the capital, until the city of Columbus — Ohio's current capital — took this honor in 1816.

Ohio's early years saw dramatic population increases as well as a great deal of civil and military turmoil. While visiting an Ohio River island owned by Ohio tycoon Harman Blennerhassett, former U.S. Vice President Aaron Burr allegedly worked on a plan to create a personal empire stretching from Ohio to Mexico, a plot for which he would stand trial for treason in 1807. (Burr was ultimately acquitted of these charges.) The great Shawnee chief Tecumseh tried to rally native people near Greenville, Ohio, into taking a last stand against the white settlers, only to be defeated in 1811 by U.S. Army General William Henry Harrison in the Battle of Tippecanoe. Harrison would later become the ninth U. S. president.

Abolition and the Civil War

Prior to the Civil War, many Ohio citizens strongly favored the abolition of slavery; these people became known as abolitionists. The Underground Railroad, a grass-roots abolitionist movement that helped escaped slaves reach freedom in Canada, was active on Lake Erie and along the Ohio River. In 1848 Ohio repealed its Black Laws, which had restricted the civil rights of African Americans. After the Civil War began, Ohio contributed about 345,000 troops to the Union army. Some Ohioans sympathized with the Confederacy (the alliance of southern states that allowed slavery); they lived mostly in southern and north–central Ohio and were known as "Copperheads."

World War I

After the United States entered World War I in 1917, Ohio turned much of its considerable industrial capacity to the war effort. Some 250,000 Ohioans enlisted in the fighting, and military training took place at Camp Sherman (for soldiers) and Dayton's Fairfield Air Depot (for pilots). Pilot Eddie Rickenbacker, who hailed from Columbus, shot down more enemy planes than any other World War I pilot. Newton D. Baker, a Cleveland resident, became President Woodrow Wilson's secretary of war during this conflict.

Ohioans in the Civil War

Ohio was the birthplace of many famous Civil War leaders, including Ulysses S. Grant (who was born in Point Pleasant), William T. Sherman (who hailed from Lancaster), and Edwin M. Stanton (of Steubenville). Ohio supplied about 345,000 Union army soldiers, more than the total quotas requested by the federal government. The Civil War spilled onto Ohio soil when Confederate General John Hunt Morgan led a cavalry raid into the state on July 13, 1863. This brief invasion ended thirteen days later when Hunt and his men surrendered at Salineville and were jailed as common horse thieves. (Morgan later escaped and returned to the South.) This incident represented the northernmost point reached by Civil War hostilities.

▶ During the Great Depression the WPA organized workers in Ohio and other states around skill groups.

Economic Upheavals

Warren G. Harding of Marion became the twenty-ninth U.S. president in 1921, after defeating Ohio's governor, James M. Cox of Dayton. Harding's proud home state experienced considerable prosperity during his presidency and throughout the 1920s. Businesses continued to flourish and expand, particularly in such fast-growing industrial centers as Cincinnati, Cleveland, Dayton, and Toledo. Farmland bordering these and other cities was quickly gobbled up by the cities' rapid expansion.

With the onset of the Great Depression in 1929, Ohio's prosperity abruptly ended. All over the United States and around the world, economies were collapsing. The once-rich

The War Between The States That Wasn't

■ In 1835 an old border dispute between Ohio and the Territory of Michigan flared up, leading to the "Toledo War" because both states claimed the Toledo area. Before the Ohio and Michigan state militias actually came to blows, President Andrew Jackson sent agents to Toledo to negotiate a truce between the governors of Ohio and Michigan. In 1836 Congress awarded the Toledo area, about 520 square miles (1,350 sq km) bordering Lake Erie, to Ohio; in return, Michigan was given the Upper Peninsula.

industrial centers of Ohio were among the state's hardest-hit areas, as factories closed and thousands of workers lost their jobs. Farmers suffered as well, with many losing their lands because of sharp drops in farm prices. At the instigation of President Franklin Delano Roosevelt, the federal government soon established jobs programs, such as the Works Progress Administration (WPA). These programs greatly helped Ohio and other financially devastated states throughout the 1930s as they struggled to recover from the economic troubles of the Depression years.

In 1934 construction began on the Muskingum River Valley flood-control project, which became nationally famous in 1937 after most of its dams withstood heavy flooding from the overflowing Ohio River. This ambitious project was finally completed in 1938. The following year Robert Alphonso Taft (1889–1953) — the son of President William Howard Taft — began his first term as a Republican senator from Ohio. He would later become one of the most powerful members of the U.S. Senate.

World War II and The Postwar Years

After the United States entered World War II in December of 1941, Ohio's industrial base once again got busy producing badly needed wartime materials such as aircraft, ships, guns, steel, and tires. The military established several new training centers across the state. Ohio's industrial output helped the eventual Allied victory in 1945. Following the war Ohio entered an unprecedented era of prosperity, as did the rest of the United States. The decades ahead, however, would pose many difficult economic and environmental challenges. True to their state motto that "all things are possible," however, Ohioans would face those challenges unflinchingly.

▼ A memorial to Commodore Perry's victory at Put-in-Bay during the War of 1812 stands on South Bass Island.

Diverse People in a Diverse Land

> No colony in America was settled under circumstances more favorable. There never were people better able to promote the welfare of the community.
> — *George Washington, on the 1788 founding of Marietta, Ohio's first town*

Multitudes in a Small Space

Although Ohio is not a very large state geographically, it contains a vast number of people — 11,353,140, according to the 2000 Census. This places Ohio seventh among the states in terms of population. Between 1990 and 2000, however, Ohio's population increased by only 4.7 percent, considerably below the national average of 13.2 percent. The reasons for this slow growth include low birth rates and high levels of migration out of the state during recent years. Fourteen of Ohio's eighty-eight counties actually lost population between 1990 and 1999. Only six states experienced slower population growth.

DID YOU KNOW?

Between 1820 and 1900 Ohio had the nation's third-largest population. Because of faster growth in other regions of the country, however, Ohio now ranks as only the seventh most populous U.S. state.

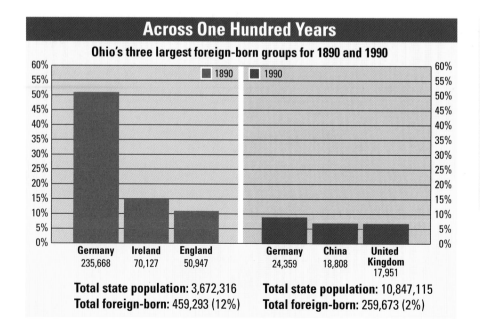

Across One Hundred Years

Ohio's three largest foreign-born groups for 1890 and 1990

☐ 1890   ■ 1990

Germany	Ireland	England
235,668	70,127	50,947

Germany	China	United Kingdom
24,359	18,808	17,951

Total state population: 3,672,316
Total foreign-born: 459,293 (12%)

Total state population: 10,847,115
Total foreign-born: 259,673 (2%)

Patterns of Immigration

The total number of people who immigrated to Ohio in 1998 was 7,697. Of that number the largest immigrant groups were from India (11%), China (6%), and Mexico (4%).

A History of Ohio's Immigrants

In the nineteenth century Ohio's population grew at a very rapid rate. Following the end of the War of 1812, settlers flooded into Ohio from the eastern states, with a great many coming from New York, Pennsylvania, and the New England states. Germany and Britain provided a considerable number of new immigrants as well. Later, in the aftermath of the Irish potato famine (1845–1849), Ireland also became a source of new Ohioans.

A Study in Diversity

The varied population of modern-day Ohio includes people descended from the settlers of the original thirteen colonies, as well as those who can trace their lineage to more recent

Age Distribution Among Ohioans	
0–4	754,930
5–9	816,346
10–14	827,811
15–19	816,868
20–24	728,928
25–44	3,325,210
45–64	2,575,290
65 and over	1,507,757

Heritage and Background, Ohio   Year 2000

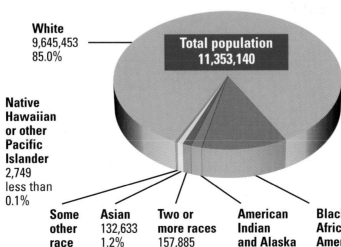

▶ Here's a look at the racial backgrounds of Ohioans today, who are predominantly of European extraction. In the 2000 Census only 1.4% of Ohio's residents reported belonging to more than one racial group.

White 9,645,453 85.0%

Total population 11,353,140

Native Hawaiian or other Pacific Islander 2,749 less than 0.1%

Some other race 88,627 0.8%

Asian 132,633 1.2%

Two or more races 157,885 1.4%

American Indian and Alaska Native 24,486 0.2%

Black or African American 1,301,307 11.5%

Note: 1.9% (217,123) of the population identify themselves as **Hispanic** or **Latino,** a cultural designation that crosses racial lines. Hispanics and Latinos are counted in this category and the racial category of their choice.

immigrants, such as the Germans and Irish. The urbanization that swept Ohio beginning in the late nineteenth century attracted large numbers of African Americans as well as people from eastern and southern Europe. Currently Ohio's black population represents about 11.5 percent of the state's general population. And although Ohio's Asian population is small, it is growing quickly.

Today more Amish reside in Ohio than in any other state. They live simply, without the use of electricity, telephones, or automobiles, just as their ancestors did in the eighteenth and nineteenth centuries.

Educational Levels of Ohio Workers	
Less than 9th grade	.546,954
9th to 12th grade, no diploma	.1,137,934
High school graduate, including equivalency	.2,515,987
Some college, no degree	.1,179,409
Associate degree	.369,144
Bachelor's degree	.767,845
Graduate or professional degree	.407,491

Where Do Ohioans Live?

About 80 percent of Ohio's residents live in the state's metropolitan areas, although many of these people do not live inside the central cities. The most densely inhabited urban areas in Ohio are Akron, Cincinnati, Cleveland,

▼ Cincinnati sits across the Ohio River from Kentucky.

Columbus (the capital), Dayton, Toledo, and Youngstown. During recent decades significant numbers of people have moved from the inner cities to the suburbs. Except for Columbus, the populations of all seven of Ohio's largest cities declined after 1970.

Education

Ohio is a fairly well-educated state, with 86.2 percent of the adults over age twenty-five holding a high school diploma and 21.5 percent having either bachelor's or advanced college degrees. The state boasts about 72,200 elementary school teachers and approximately 36,100 secondary school instructors, who earn an average salary of $38,600 and $39,800 respectively. Ohio spends more than $13.5 billion annually on public education, which breaks down to $1,206 per capita, or $6,539 per pupil (based on 1998 figures).

▲ A student at Indian Hill High School uses laboratory equipment.

Ohio's median age is 36.2, which is relatively "old" in comparison with other highly populous states. This contrasts sharply with such states as California and Arizona, whose median ages are 33.3 and 34.2 respectively. Ohio's median age is one year higher than the national average. At 51.8 percent of the state's total, the female population slightly outnumbers the males, who make up 48.2 percent of the total population.

Religion

Early Ohio settlers from New England brought with them their Puritan and Congregationalist faiths. Throughout the nineteenth century people who belonged to other Protestant groups — Baptists, Episcopalians, Methodists, Presbyterians, and Universalists — took up residence within the state. Smaller religious groups, such as the Amish, Moravians, Quakers, and Zoarites, also made Ohio their home. Today Ohio boasts a tremendous variety of religious faiths. Most of these are Christian, with non-Christians such as Jews (1.2 percent of the population), Muslims (0.4 percent), and Buddhist (0.1 percent) represented as well, primarily in urban areas.

Forests, Soil, and Steel

> The Ohio Country is fine, rich, level land, well-timbered with large walnut, ash, sugar trees. . . . It is well watered . . . and full of beautiful natural . . . meadows, abounding with turkeys, deer, elk, and most sorts of game, particularly buffaloes. In short, it wants nothing but cultivation to make it a most delightful country.
>
> — *George Gist, 18th-century representative of the Ohio Company of Virginia*

Ancient glaciers sculpted much of the land we now call Ohio, carved out Lake Erie, and changed the course of the area's rivers. These irresistible forces also gave rise to some of the nation's most fertile farmland and Ohio's other abundant natural resources. During more recent centuries Ohio's landscape has been re-shaped nearly as profoundly by human hands.

Climate

Ohio has warm, humid summers and cold winters, with seasonal temperature averages varying by 45 degrees. This climate is typical of Ohio's eastern, mid-latitude location, although cyclonic weather systems in the westerly wind belt keep the weather varied. The state's average annual precipitation (rain, snowmelt, hail, and other moisture) is 38 inches (97 centimeters), and occurs throughout the year. Summers are generally somewhat wetter than autumns. Ohio's southwest region receives the most precipitation,

DID YOU KNOW?

Ohio has more than 180 artificially created lakes, each one covering an area of at least 40 acres (16 hectares).

▼ *From left to right:* **Amish country in the winter; Cucumber Falls; fertile farmland; an Ohio coal mine; Cleveland skyline; Cuyahoga National Recreation Area.**

while the northeastern area along Lake Erie (between Sandusky and Toledo) receives the least.

Resources

When European explorers first arrived in Ohio, they encountered a few small patches of open prairie scattered amid giant tracts of forest. Today nearly half of Ohio's total land area is used for agriculture, while urbanized areas occupy a large area as well. Fertile, glacier-deposited soils — sometimes several feet deep — can be found in all parts of Ohio except the southeast, where the ancient, earth-moving glaciers never reached.

Some of Ohio's soils include such useful industrial and building materials as limestone, sandstone, and shale. Large deposits of clay, sand and gravel, peat, and gypsum are also plentiful. Coal, however, is the most important product taken from the ground in Ohio. Coal deposits in the east and southeast — ranging from Geauga County in the north to Lawrence County in the south — are estimated at 24 billion tons. Ohio also has oil and natural gas reserves, which can be found in various locations throughout the state. This includes about 100 million barrels in crude oil reserves. Northeast Ohio contains vast reserves of rock salt as well and could supply the entire nation with salt for many thousands of years.

Water, Water, All Around

Water is one of Ohio's most critical natural resources because the state is one of the nation's largest water users. Ninety-five percent of the water Ohio consumes comes from surface supplies, including Lake Erie.

Ohio's rivers and streams flow, for the most part, south into the Ohio River, or north into Lake Erie. A drainage divide (known as "Ohio's backbone" and consisting of low hills) determines in which direction a given stream will

Average January temperature
Cleveland: 27°F (-2.78°C)
Cincinnati: 30°F (-1.11°C)

Average July temperature
Cleveland: 73°F (22.78°C)
Cincinnati: 76°F (24.44°C)

Average yearly rainfall
Cleveland: 36.63 inches (93 cm)
Cincinnati: 41.33 inches (105 cm)

Average yearly snowfall
Cleveland: 55.4 inches (140.7 cm)
Cincinnati: 23.2 inches (58.9 cm)

Major Rivers

Ohio River
981 miles (1,579 km) long; 450 miles (724 km) along Ohio's border

Scioto River
237 miles (381 km) long

Muskingum River
115 miles (185 km) long

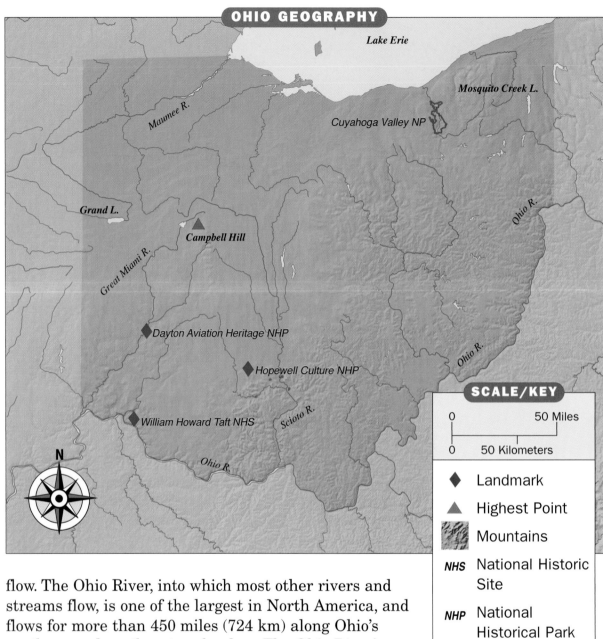

Lake Erie

Mosquito Creek L.

Maumee R.

Cuyahoga Valley NP

Grand L.

Ohio R.

Campbell Hill

Great Miami R.

Dayton Aviation Heritage NHP

Hopewell Culture NHP

Ohio R.

William Howard Taft NHS

Scioto R.

Ohio R.

N

SCALE/KEY

0	50 Miles
0	50 Kilometers

◆ Landmark

▲ Highest Point

▨ Mountains

NHS National Historic Site

NHP National Historical Park

NP National Park

flow. The Ohio River, into which most other rivers and streams flow, is one of the largest in North America, and flows for more than 450 miles (724 km) along Ohio's southern and southeastern borders. The Ohio River's longest tributary in Ohio is the Scioto River, which extends 237 miles (381 km).

Ohio's lakes include the 3,457 square miles (8,954 sq km) covered by Lake Erie, which straddles the International Line between the United States and Canada. Lake Erie's 312-mile (502-km) shoreline area in Ohio supports a profusion of harbors and recreation areas. Ohio has more than 2,500 lakes larger than 2 acres (0.8 ha), over twenty of which are natural, glacier-formed lakes with areas of 40 acres (16 ha) or more.

Highest Elevation
Campbell Hill
1,550 feet (472 m)

Lowest Elevation
Ohio River
433 feet (132 m)

Plants and Wildlife

In pre-Columbian times Ohio's vegetation was comprised of mixed hardwood forests, which all but covered the state. The northwestern lake plain included the swamp forest (or Black Swamp), and the west central part of Ohio supported scattered prairie grasslands. More than five centuries later, settlement and intensive land use have greatly altered these habitats. Today about one quarter of Ohio is forest, in varying stages of re-growth. Most of the trees are hardwoods, such as beeches, black walnuts, hickories, maples, sycamores, red and white oaks, tulip trees, white ashes, and white elms. Azalea, dogwood, hawthorn, sumac, and viburnum are among Ohio's most common shrubs. Among the state's wildflowers are anemones, blazing stars, blue sages, Indian pipes, lilies, saxifrages, toothworts, and wild indigos.

Animals Abound

Ohio has few large wild animals, and of these only white-tailed deer are plentiful, although a few black bears can still be found. Among Ohio's smaller wild animals are minks, muskrats, opossums, cottontail rabbits, raccoons, red foxes, skunks, weasels, and wild turkeys; the wide distribution of these animals allows trapping in rural areas. Ohio's varied wildlife supports a significant amount of recreational hunting in some two hundred fifty designated public areas. Wild ducks (common in the marshes along Lake Erie), geese, pheasants, quail, and ruffed grouse number among the game birds; the ring-necked pheasant and Hungarian partridge are non-native species that have been introduced into Ohio. Ohio's predominant fish include black bass, walleyed pike, Ohio muskellunge, white bass, perch, saugers, bluegills, rock bass, and channel catfish. The state's songbirds include blackbirds, brown thrashers, cardinals, chickadees, and wrens.

Largest Lakes

Lake Erie
241 miles (388 km) long
57 miles (92 km) wide at widest point
Average depth of 62 feet (19 m)
Maximum depth of 210 feet (64 m)

Mosquito Creek Lake (reservoir)
12 sq miles (31 sq km) in area

Grand Lake
9 miles (14.5 km) long
4 miles (6.4 km) wide at widest point
21.1 sq miles (54.6 sq km) in area

◀ The wood duck, near extinction in North America in the early 1900s, was the target of a recovery project sponsored by the U.S Department of Agriculture beginning in 1917. Today wood ducks are among Ohio's most numerous waterfowl.

Ohio: A State on the Move

> Where the Cuyahoga River flows
> into Lake Erie shall rise a community
> of vast commercial importance.
>
> — *George Washington, speaking in 1765*
> *of what would one day become Cleveland*

A Revolution in Transportation

With the Louisiana Purchase of 1803, Ohioans quickly began a thriving trade with New Orleans via the Mississippi River. As the nineteenth century progressed, so did the pace of travel for Ohio's people and goods. In 1811 the *New Orleans,* a wood-burning side-wheeler, became the first steamboat to navigate the Ohio River. In 1818 the steamboat *Walks-in-the-Water* went from Buffalo to Cleveland, becoming the first vessel of its kind to travel Lake Erie, and established the Great Lakes as a commercial shipping link between the eastern and western United States. The National (or Cumberland) Road, built between 1811 and 1841, ran from Maryland through Columbus to Illinois. Ohio's goods and resources found ever wider distribution thanks to the Erie Canal (completed in 1825, it connected Lake Erie with New York City), the Ohio & Erie Canal (completed in 1832, it joins Cleveland and Portsmouth), and the Miami–Erie Canal (completed in 1845, it connects Toledo with Cincinnati). In 1832 Ohio's first railroad was built, although major lines were not constructed until the 1850s.

Innovation After the Civil War

Ohio grew into an industrial and agricultural giant after the U.S. Civil War (1861–1865), with workers from all over the world moving to the state. In 1870 Benjamin F. Goodrich opened his first rubber factory in Akron, a development that would one day make Ohio one of the world's principal sources of rubber products. The same year John D. Rockefeller established the Standard Oil Company

DID YOU KNOW?

As a result of industrial pollution, the Cuyahoga River actually burst into flames in 1936! Later fires on the Cuyahoga helped inspire the Clean Water Act, the Great Lakes Water Quality Agreement, and the establishment of federal and state Environmental Protection Agencies.

Top Employers

(of workers age sixteen and over; totals add up to more than 100% as some residents hold more than one job)

Service industries (restaurants, hotels, etc.)	31%
Manufacturing	23%
Wholesale or retail trade	22%
Government	12%
Transportation, communication, and utilities	6.0%
Finance, insurance, and real estate	5.7%
Construction	5.0%
Agriculture	1.8%
Mining	20%

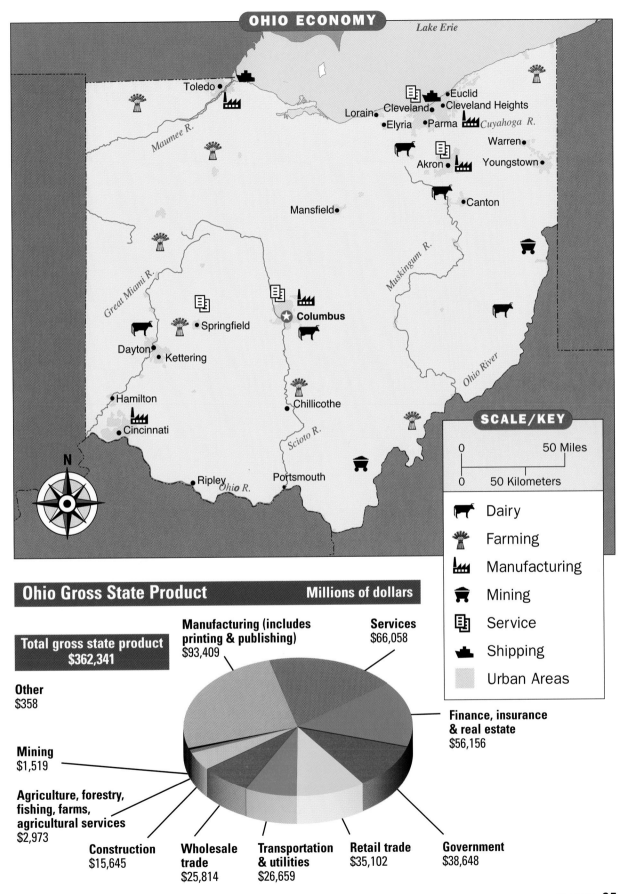

OHIO ECONOMY

Lake Erie

Toledo

Lorain • Euclid
Cleveland • Cleveland Heights
Elyria • Parma *Cuyahoga R.*
Warren
Akron • Youngstown

Maumee R.

Mansfield

Canton

Muskingum R.

Great Miami R.

Springfield

Columbus

Dayton • Kettering

Ohio River

Chillicothe

Hamilton

Cincinnati

Scioto R.

Ripley
Ohio R. Portsmouth

SCALE/KEY

0 ——— 50 Miles

0 ——— 50 Kilometers

🐄 Dairy
🌾 Farming
🏭 Manufacturing
🛒 Mining
📇 Service
🚢 Shipping
▫️ Urban Areas

Ohio Gross State Product

Millions of dollars

Total gross state product $362,341

Manufacturing (includes printing & publishing) $93,409

Services $66,058

Other $358

Finance, insurance & real estate $56,156

Mining $1,519

Agriculture, forestry, fishing, farms, agricultural services $2,973

Government $38,648

Construction $15,645

Wholesale trade $25,814

Transportation & utilities $26,659

Retail trade $35,102

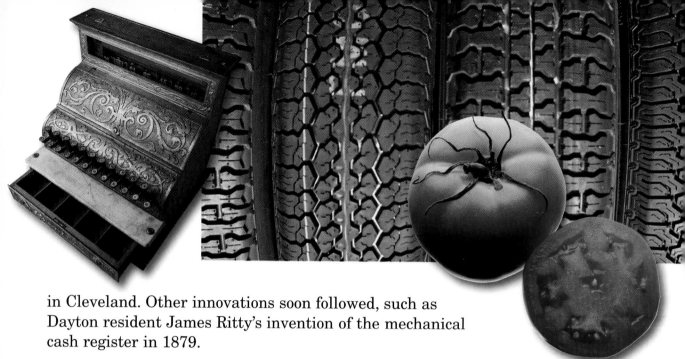

in Cleveland. Other innovations soon followed, such as Dayton resident James Ritty's invention of the mechanical cash register in 1879.

Labor Strife and Reform

The prominence of industry in Ohio led to the state's important role in the labor movement of the nineteenth century. The American Federation of Labor was formed in Columbus in 1886, and the United Mine Workers was established in 1888. In the mining regions of southeastern Ohio, labor unrest became common, as did outbreaks of violence between workers and management. During an 1884 strike several mine shafts in Perry County were set ablaze — and continue burning to this day!

Boom Times: The 1950s and 1960s

In the prosperous 1950s the U.S. Atomic Energy Commission (AEC) built several installations in Ohio, including Pike County's Portsmouth Area Project, a producer of the uranium-235 used in nuclear reactors. In 1958 Cleveland's Lewis Field became the site of the John H. Glenn Research Center, an installation established by the National Aeronautics and Space Administration (NASA). The Glenn Center is dedicated to advanced research on space propulsion systems and is named after one of Ohio's most famous sons, John Glenn, the first American to orbit Earth.

Ohio's industrial and business growth continued unabated into the 1960s. The state became involved in international trade as eight Lake Erie-based cities — Ashtabula, Cleveland, Conneaut, Fairport, Huron, Lorain, Sandusky, and Toledo — became ports of the St. Lawrence

▲ Ohio has contributed innovations like the cash register to modern life. Rubber for tires and top crops like tomatoes drive the state's economy.

Made in Ohio

Leading farm products and crops
Celery
Corn
Dairy products
Grapes
Hay
Soybeans
Tomatoes

Other products
Crushed stone
Electrical equipment
Machine tools
Rubber
Salt
Steel
Transportation
  equipment

Seaway, which opened for shipping traffic in 1959. By 1970 Ohio ranked fourth among U.S. states in the value of its annual exports. Inexpensive, coal-generated power encouraged the construction of many new aluminum factories and chemical plants in cities along the Ohio River.

Modern Ohio's Products and Services

Today, as for more than a century, Ohio's chief products come from its agricultural, manufacturing, and mining industries. The state's farmers produce corn, soybeans, hay, wheat, oats, potatoes, tomatoes, grapes, and many other products. The manufacturing sector satisfies much of the nation's need for steel, machine tools, automobile parts, rubber, transportation equipment, electrical equipment, paper, and ships. Ohio's mining companies provide vast quantities of crushed stone, salt, construction sand and gravel, limestone, and natural gas.

Economic Problems

Ohio's economy is sensitive to the effects of foreign competition, fluctuations in energy prices and supplies, factory relocations, and recession (the shrinking of the overall size of the economy). All of these factors have devastated Ohio's industrial inner cities during recent decades. Also greatly affected are the Appalachian plateau's coal miners, who suffer from chronic poverty and unemployment. Additionally, declining crop and livestock prices have forced many small farmers out of business. As a result of the manufacturing job-losses and plant closures of the 1970s and 1980s, Ohio and other nearby states became known collectively as the "Rust Belt."

Despite these problems, Ohio still struggles to remain at the forefront of the nation's heavy industry. Fortunately, these declines have been offset recently by the arrival of Japanese-owned manufacturing plants in Ohio.

Ohio: The Birthplace of Mass Production

Henry Ford is generally credited with the invention of the mass-production assembly line, but a direct ancestor to this process can be traced to the nineteenth-century meat-packing plants of Cincinnati. There, workers used overhead trolleys to move animal carcasses from worker to worker. When these trolleys were equipped with engine-driven chains, they constituted a kind of "assembly line," allowing each worker to concentrate on a single task while the machinery set the pace.

International Airports		
Airport	Location	Passengers per year (approx)
Hopkins International	Cleveland	13,288,059
Cincinnati/Northern Kentucky International	Cincinnati	11,203,192
Port Columbus International	Columbus	6,838,047

The Moderate Middle

> We have got rid of the fetish of the divine right of kings, and that slavery is of divine origin and authority.
>
> — *From the diary of former U.S. president Rutherford B. Hayes, March 1, 1890*

A New State

On March 1, 1803, Ohio became the Union's seventeenth state. Edward Tiffin, a member of the Democratic-Republican party, served as the new state's first governor. Chillicothe became the state capital until 1810, when it was moved to Zanesville. In 1812 Chillicothe again became the capital until 1816, when Columbus became the location of Ohio's capital, where it remains today.

Ohio's Constitution

The current constitution of Ohio was adopted in 1851, replacing the state's original constitution. The constitution may be amended by means of a proposal by the state legislature, a petition signed by one-tenth of Ohio's voters, or by constitutional convention. A convention may be called

Ohio State Constitution

"All men are, by nature, free and independent, and have certain inalienable rights, among which are those of enjoying and defending life and liberty, acquiring, possessing, and protecting property, and seeking and obtaining happiness and safety."

—1851

Elected Posts in the Executive Branch

Office	Length of Term	Term Limits
Governor	4 years	2 consecutive terms in 12 years
Lieutenant Governor	4 years	2 consecutive terms in 12 years
Attorney General	4 years	2 consecutive terms in 12 years
Secretary of State	4 years	2 consecutive terms in 12 years
Auditor	4 years	2 consecutive terms in 12 years
Treasurer	4 years	2 consecutive terms in 12 years

DID YOU KNOW?

Two Ohioan U.S. presidents also served as governors of their native state: Rutherford B. Hayes (who was Ohio's chief executive from 1868 to 1876) and William McKinley (who was governor from 1892 to 1896).

only if approved by two-thirds of both houses of the legislature and by a majority of the electorate. All constitutional amendments must be approved by a majority of the state's voters.

Executive Branch

Ohio's chief executive officer is the governor, who is elected by voters to a four-year term. There is no limit to the number of terms a governor may serve, but no governor may serve more than two consecutive terms (the same rule applies to the offices of lieutenant governor, secretary of state, attorney general, treasurer, and auditor). The governor has the authority to appoint the heads of many state agencies, as well as the trustees of state-subsidized universities and other institutions. The state Senate must approve all of the governor's appointments.

Legislative Branch

Ohio's legislature, known as the General Assembly, is made up of a Senate and a House of Representatives. Voters in

▼ Construction of the Ohio state capitol building in Columbus began in 1838 and was completed in 1861.

each senatorial district elect one senator to serve a four-year term. State representatives serve two-year terms. The General Assembly goes into session on the first Monday in January of each odd-numbered year, and there are no set time limits for the duration of a session.

Judicial Branch

Ohio's highest court is called the Supreme Court. It consists of seven justices, all of whom are elected to six-year terms. The state also has twelve courts of appeals. Ohio's highest trial courts are called the courts of common pleas, and each of Ohio's eighty-eight counties has one such court. These judges are also elected to six-year terms, and the number serving on each court varies. Other Ohio courts include county, municipal, juvenile, mayoral, and probate courts.

Party Politics

During the late nineteenth century, Ohio's government was beset by public scandals. Political "bosses" such as Marcus A. "Mark" Hannah (a Cleveland Republican) and George B. Cox (a Cincinnati Republican) essentially controlled state politics. Political reform movements began taking hold throughout the nation around 1900, promoting integrity and efficiency in city and state governments. Cincinnati's William Howard Taft became the nation's twenty-seventh president in 1909 and carried similar reforms into the private sector. Taft aggressively took on powerful business monopolies and championed the cause of conservation of natural resources.

Robert James Harlan was a former slave from Harrodsburg, Kentucky, who grew up on a farm owned by the father of Supreme Court Justice James Marshall Harlan. The Harlan family educated Robert, and he left as a young man to seek his fortune in California during the Gold Rush of 1848. He returned having made at least $50,000 and bought his freedom for $500. Once he gained his freedom, he moved to Cincinnati, where he went into real estate, opened a photography studio, and built the city's first school for African-American children. During the Civil War he raised a battalion of four hundred African Americans and was commissioned as a colonel. He returned to Cincinnati and in 1886 was elected to the state legislature, where he fought to repeal the state's "black laws" — laws that permitted discrimination and segregation.

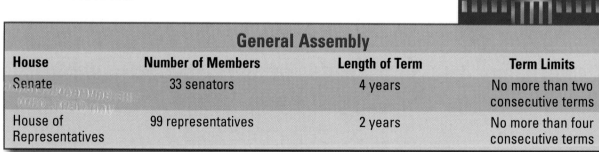

General Assembly			
House	Number of Members	Length of Term	Term Limits
Senate	33 senators	4 years	No more than two consecutive terms
House of Representatives	99 representatives	2 years	No more than four consecutive terms

The White House via Ohio

Seven Ohio-born leaders have assumed the presidency of the United States:

ULYSSES S. GRANT (1869–1877)
A member of the Republican party, Grant was born in Point Pleasant and served as commander in chief of the Union army during the Civil War. He became the eighteenth U.S. president in 1869.

RUTHERFORD B. HAYES (1877–1881)
Born in Delaware, Ohio, and a Republican party member, Hayes served as the nineteenth U.S. president. He ended Reconstruction in the South.

JAMES ABRAM GARFIELD (1881)
A Republican born in Cuyahoga County, Garfield was elected as the twentieth U.S. president but was shot and died only months into his term.

BENJAMIN HARRISON (1889–1893)
Born in North Bend, Republican Benjamin Harrison (grandson of ninth president William Henry Harrison) served as the twenty-third U.S. president.

WILLIAM MCKINLEY (1897–1901)
A Republican from Niles, McKinley was the twenty-fifth U.S. president. He was assassinated at the beginning of his second term.

WILLIAM HOWARD TAFT (1909–1913)
This Cincinnati-born Republican served as the twenty-seventh U.S. president.
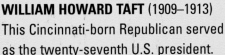

WARREN G. HARDING (1921–1923)
A Republican born in Corsica, Harding was the twenty-ninth president of the United States. He died while in office.

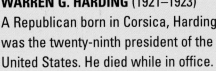

In Ohio both the Democratic and Republican parties are highly influential. Cleveland and other northeastern cities tend to be Democratic strongholds, while the Republicans hold sway in Cincinnati, Columbus, and most rural regions. Since 1945 candidates from both major parties have won Ohio's governorship in more or less equal numbers.

Ohio is frequently regarded as a political bellwether for the rest of nation, meaning that the political beliefs of Ohioans are usually a fairly good indicator of the political mood of the country as a whole; the winners of most of the presidential races of the last two centuries have won Ohio's electoral votes.

Beauty Amid Coal and Steel

> Beautiful Ohio, where the golden grain
> Dwarf the lovely flowers in the summer rain.
> Cities rising high, silhouette the sky.
> Freedom is supreme in this majestic land;
> Mighty factories seem to hum in tune, so grand.
> Beautiful Ohio, thy wonders are in view,
> Land where my dreams all come true!
>
> — *Ohio's official state song, "Beautiful Ohio," composed by Mary Earl, with lyrics by Ballard MacDonald and Wilbert B. McBride*

Cultural activities are extremely important to Ohioans. The state boasts some of the world's finest universities, libraries, orchestras, and museums, as well as world-class sports venues and countless other points of educational, cultural, and historical appeal. Ohio's cultural interests include not only the sublime artistic achievements of several metropolitan symphony orchestras, but also embrace popular culture. In 1985 Rick Derringer's "Hang On Sloopy" became the state's official state rock-and-roll song. Ohio natives have contributed greatly to American culture; the cowboy crooner Roy Rogers and actors Clark Gable, Lillian Gish, Paul Newman, and Doris Day all hailed from Ohio.

The Arts

The Cleveland Orchestra is widely regarded as one of the world's best symphony orchestras. In winter this fine orchestra makes its home at Severance Hall; in summer it performs at Blossom Music Center, located in the valley between Cleveland and Akron. The Cincinnati Symphony Orchestra is also highly respected for its artistic achievements. Ohio excels in the worlds of live theater and dance. The Karamu House and Theatre in Cleveland is well known for its innovative productions of multicultural plays and dance programs.

DID YOU KNOW?

The name "hot dog" for a frankfurter, or weiner, originated in Ohio. After Harry M. Stevens of Niles saw a cartoon portraying a dachshund as a wiener, he coined the term "hot dog" to describe the time-honored wiener-in-a-bun sandwich.

Ohio's decision to adopt an official rock-and-roll song makes the state the perfect home for Cleveland's Rock and Roll Hall of Fame and Museum. This non-profit museum chronicles rock and roll's tumultuous half-century of development and contains interactive exhibits, films, videos, and unique rock-era artifacts. In addition to the permanent Hall of Fame exhibits, the museum also stages temporary exhibits throughout the year. The Rock and Roll Hall of Fame maintains a regular schedule of lectures, panel discussions, and concerts. The Hall of Fame has been nominating and inducting performers, composers, disk jockeys, and other influential figures from the world of rock and roll since 1986.

The Rock and Roll Hall of Fame and Museum

Housed within one of the designs of internationally renowned architect I. M. Pei, the Rock and Roll Hall of Fame and Museum offers interactive exhibits, films and videos, as well as priceless and poignant artifacts of the rock-and-roll era. Among the items on display are one of John Lennon's school report cards and Jim Morrison's Cub Scout uniform. The Rock and Roll Hall of Fame and Museum is located in downtown Cleveland, on the shores of Lake Erie. The Rock and Roll Hall of Fame honors the legendary performers, producers, songwriters, disc jockeys, and others who have made rock and roll the vital cultural force that it remains today.

▼ Severance Hall in Cleveland, home to the Cleveland Orchestra.

Painting, Sculpture, and the Graphic Arts

Ohio's large cities are well known for products other than steel, glass, or rubber; they are also some of the nation's most vibrant art centers. The Columbus Museum of Art, established in 1878, was the first art museum to open in Ohio. It exhibits the work of noted Ohio painters Elijah Pierce and George Bellows, and it is also the home of the world-famous Howald Collection of early modern painting. The Cincinnati Art Museum showcases statuary from the Greek and Roman periods, other works dating back to ancient Egypt, and contains a substantial collection of European paintings from the seventeenth through the twentieth centuries. The Taft Museum, also in Cincinnati, spotlights a diverse collection of paintings by master artists, Chinese porcelains, and other unique antiquities. Cincinnati's Contemporary Arts Center (founded in 1939) is one of the nation's oldest and most innovative contemporary art museums.

In 1990 the CAC gained international attention when it successfully defended its legal right to exhibit — and its audience's legal right to view — the controversial photography of Robert Mapplethorpe.

The Cleveland Museum of Art is especially notable for its medieval European and Asian art collections. In Toledo, long known as the "glass capital of the world," the Toledo Museum of Art features an abundance of glass artwork and has a general art collection containing more than thirty thousand works, including European and American paintings and Greek vases. The Akron Art Museum, housed in a renovated post office building, emphasizes folk art, contemporary art, and photography. The Dayton Art Institute boasts a large Asian and African art collection. The Allen Memorial Art Museum at Oberlin College features modern European and contemporary American art, Renaissance and Baroque prints, and seventeenth-century Dutch and Japanese prints.

In addition to museums that display world art masterworks, Ohio also has produced some world-class artists of its own. Maya Ying Lin (1960) of Athens designed the Vietnam Veterans Memorial, the striking black granite monument in Washington, D.C., that bears the names of the 58,000 Americans who died or were missing during the Vietnam War.

▲ The first nine members of the Cincinnati Red Stockings Baseball Club in 1869. They were the first fully professional baseball team.

◀ The Cleveland Museum of Art.

Literature

Ohio has also had its share of literary giants, including William Sydney Porter (1862–1910), who is better known by his pen name O. Henry. Porter produced a large body of short stories, including "The Ransom of Red Chief" and "The Gift of the Magi", which are still widely read today and whose "twist endings" are still widely imitated. James Thurber (1894–1961) of Columbus was a world-famous humorist and cartoonist whose works encompassed everything from children's books to cartoons and stories for *The New Yorker.* Ohioan Ambrose Bierce (1842–1914) was the author of many classic Civil War stories, including "An Occurrence at Owl Creek Bridge." Paul Laurence Dunbar (1872–1906), a prominent African-American poet (author of the collection *Oak and Ivy*), was born in Milan, the son of a slave. Abolitionist Harriet Beecher Stowe (1811–1896) lived for many years in Cincinnati and wrote the classic antislavery novel, *Uncle Tom's Cabin.* Nobel Prize-winning African-American author Toni Morrison (1931) also hails from Ohio, as did Western genre novelist Zane Gray (1875–1939), renowned fantasist and science-fiction writer Harlan Ellison (1934), influential book reviewer William Dean Howells (1837–1920), and children's authors Lois Lenski (1893–1974), Robert McCloskey (1914), Robin McKinley (1952), Virginia Hamilton (1936), and R. L. Stine (1943).

Publishing and Periodicals

Cincinnati was the home of the *Centinel of the North-Western Territory* (founded in 1793), the first newspaper to be published north and west of the Ohio River. The first antislavery newspaper in the United States, the *Philanthropist,* initially appeared in 1817 in Mount Pleasant. Modern-day Ohio supports about eighty daily newspapers and approximately 260 weeklies. The largest of the dailies include the *Cleveland Plain Dealer*, Akron's *Beacon Journal*, the Toledo *Blade, The Columbus Dispatch, The Cincinnati Post*, the *Cincinnati Enquirer,* and the *Dayton Daily News.*

Radio and Television

WHK, the state's oldest radio station, went on the air in Cleveland in 1922, the same year Ohio State University in Columbus established WOSU, North America's first

▼ William Sydney Porter, better known as O. Henry. His first story was written while he was in an Ohio jail for stealing money from one of his employers.

educational radio station. Ohio's first television station, Cleveland's WEWS-TV, opened in 1947. Currently some 390 radio stations and about 30 television stations operate in Ohio, with cable television service reaching across much of the state.

Sports

Ohio has several professional sports franchises. The Cincinnati Bengals and the Cleveland Browns are the state's National Football League (NFL) teams. The Pro Football Hall of Fame is in Canton. Ohio baseball fans can choose between the Cleveland Indians and the Cincinnati Reds. The Reds won the World Series in 1919, 1940, 1975, and 1990. The Indians won in 1920 and 1948. Ohio has only one National Basketball Association (NBA) team, the Cleveland Cavaliers, who have been playing since 1970. Ohio's WNBA team, the Cleveland Rockers, is named after the Rock and Roll Hall of Fame, located in Cleveland. Columbus is home to the state's only National Hockey League team, the Blue Jackets.

Education: A Life-Long Project

Ohio's first school opened in 1773 at Schoenbrunn, near present-day New Philadelphia. The state's public school system began operating in 1825, and public high schools were authorized in 1853.

Ohio also has a great many prestigious universities, such

◀ *Dempsey and Firpo* (1924), by Ohio painter George Bellows (1862–1910).

Ohio Sports Firsts

1869 — The Cincinnati Red Stockings (now the Reds) became the first fully professional U.S. baseball team, meaning that all their players were paid.

1870 — The Cincinnati Red Stockings finished their first season of professional play, winning their first eighty-four games. The Red Stockings' success led to the end of amateur teams and the rise of professional teams.

1871 — The National Association of Base-Ball Players (later the National League of Base Ball Clubs) formed, and its first official big-league baseball season opened in Cleveland.

1893 — Mount Union College became one of the first campuses in the United States to form a basketball team.

1920 — National Football League was founded in an auto showroom in Canton, Ohio. Football legend Jim Thorpe was named president of the newly formed professional league.

Sport	Team	Home
Baseball	Cincinnati Reds	Cinergy Field (Riverfront Stadium), Cincinnati
	Cleveland Indians	Jacobs Field, Cleveland
Basketball	Cleveland Cavaliers	Gund Arena, Cleveland
Women's Basketball	Cleveland Rockers	Gund Arena, Cleveland
Football	Cincinnati Bengals	Paul Brown Stadium, Cincinnati
	Cleveland Browns	Browns Stadium, Cleveland
Hockey	Columbus Blue Jackets	Nationwide Arena, Columbus

as Bowling Green State University; Cleveland's Case Western Reserve University; and Oberlin College (established in 1833), which was one of the first institutions of higher learning in the nation to open its doors to women and to African-American students. Wilberforce University, a private university for African Americans, opened in 1856. The Ohio State university system has campuses in Columbus, Lima, Marion, Mansfield, and Newark and an Agricultural Technical Institute in Wooster. Ohio University, which opened in 1804, was the first public college or university in the Northwest Territory. Ohio also has an abundance of public libraries, a tradition dating back to Ohio's first subscription library in Belpre. The Cleveland Public Library is one of the biggest and most comprehensive in the nation. Cincinnati, Columbus, Dayton, Toledo, and Youngstown also enjoy extensive public libraries.

Significant library collections can also be found at Ohio State University at Columbus, which has Ohio's largest concentration of libraries. A wealth of other educational resources is available in Ohio's many museums. The Cincinnati Museum Center (which houses the Cincinnati History Museum, the Cincinnati Museum of Natural History and Science, an Omnimax Theater, and the Cincinnati Historical Society Library), the Cincinnati Zoo, the Cleveland Museum of Natural History, the Health Museum of Cleveland, the Wright-Patterson Air Force Museum, the Toledo Zoo, and Akron's EcoTarium: A Center for Environmental Exploration are only a few prominent examples.

DID YOU KNOW?

Canton, currently the site of the Pro Football Hall of Fame, has long been associated with the sport. In 1920 the National Football League (NFL) began in Canton, which was home to the Canton Bulldogs, one of the earliest professional football teams. Pioneering football star Jim Thorpe (1888–1953), one of the nation's greatest athletes, played for the Bulldogs.

The Heartland's Heart

> You might as well fall flat on your face as lean over too far backward.
>
> — *James Thurber, in the* New Yorker, *1939*

Following are only a few of the thousands of people who lived, died, or spent most of their lives in Ohio and made extraordinary contributions to the state and the nation.

TECUMSEH

NATIVE AMERICAN LEADER

BORN: *circa 1768, Old Piqua, near modern Dayton*
DIED: *October 5, 1813, Chatham, Ontario, Canada*

Tecumseh, whose name means "shooting star" or "meteor," worked to unite Ohio Native Americans to stop white expansion into their lands. Tecumseh and his brother Tenskwatawa (the "Shawnee Prophet") worked together in this effort. A gifted speaker and warrior, Tecumseh opposed Indiana Territorial Governor William Henry Harrison's 1809 treaty, an agreement that turned over much Native land to the United States and led to the Battle of Tippecanoe in November 1811 — a battle that effectively broke Tecumseh's resistance movement. Tecumseh survived to help the British fight the United States in the War of 1812 but was killed in 1813 at the Battle of the Thames in Ontario, Canada.

WILLIAM SHERMAN

MILITARY LEADER

BORN: *February 8, 1820, Lancaster*
DIED: *February 14, 1891, New York, NY*

William Tecumseh Sherman made his mark as a Union general in the Civil War. He fought in the First Battle of Bull Run (1861), the Battle of Shiloh (1862), and assisted Union victories at Vicksburg and Chattanooga (both in 1863). Sherman's troops captured and burned Atlanta, Georgia, undertook the famous "march to the sea," and cut a swath through the Carolinas (1865), burning barns, fields, and houses, breaking the Confederacy's will to fight. Sherman served as the U.S. Army's general-in-chief (1869–1883), succeeding Ulysses S. Grant. In 1884, after both major political parties had asked him to run for president, Sherman said: "I will not accept if nominated and will not serve if elected."

THOMAS EDISON

INVENTOR

BORN: *February 11, 1847, Milan*
DIED: *October 18, 1931, West Orange, NJ*

Mostly self-educated, Thomas Alva Edison became the most prolific inventor of his time. Intensely curious about the world and a voracious reader, young Edison sold magazines and candy on the Grand Trunk Railroad to buy books and equipment for his laboratory. During this time Edison suffered an accident that left him partially deaf. At the age of twenty-one, Edison used the $40,000 proceeds from his first major invention (the stock ticker) to establish a research laboratory in Newark, New Jersey, which he later relocated to Menlo Park. There, Edison and his employees created a flood of inventions, including the incandescent electric light bulb, the phonograph, the carbon microphone, the motion-picture projector, celluloid film, and the alkaline storage battery. At the time of his death, at age eighty-four, Edison held patents to 1,093 inventions.

ANNIE OAKLEY

SHARPSHOOTER

BORN: *August 13, 1860, Darke County*
DIED: *November 3, 1926, Greenville*

Born Phoebe Ann Moses, Annie Oakley was renowned for her astonishing accuracy and

▶ Annie Oakley.

speed with rifles and pistols. A hunter from the age of eight, Oakley helped support her family by hunting game for a Cincinnati hotel. At sixteen, she beat professional marksman Frank Butler in a shooting contest. Later, she married him. Oakley could shoot a playing card in half, blow a cigarette out of a man's mouth, or hit a dime in mid-air from 90 feet (27 meters) away. From 1885 to 1902 she was a leading attraction in Buffalo Bill's Wild West Show, touring the United States and Europe. Only 5 feet (1.5 m) tall, Oakley was called "Little Sure Shot" by Sioux Indian chief Sitting Bull. The popular musical *Annie Get Your Gun* (1946) is loosely based upon her life.

LILLIAN D. WALD

SOCIAL REFORMER

BORN: *March 10, 1867, Cincinnati*
DIED: *September 1, 1940, Westport, CT*

After her graduation from nursing school in 1891, Lillian D. Wald moved to New York City, where she worked to improve living conditions for the poorest residents of the city's Lower East Side. Initially, Wald worked as a visiting nurse, but by 1893 she established the Henry Street Settlement House, which catered to the needs of the poor. She later expanded this establishment into a training center for nurses. In 1902 Wald started the world's first public school nursing program in New York City. Wald also deserves much of the credit for the creation of the United States Children's Bureau, which opened in 1912. "Nursing," Wald said, "is love in action."

ART TATUM

JAZZ MUSICIAN

BORN: *October 13, 1910, Toledo*
DIED: *November 4, 1956, Los Angeles, CA*

Art Tatum was one of the first great keyboard players of the jazz age and strongly influenced the development of jazz music. Despite his near-blindness, Tatum threw himself into music at age thirteen, starting with the violin. While still in his twenties, he had become a world-renowned jazz pianist and formed his own trio in Chicago. Tatum recorded and performed extensively all over the United States and in Europe, both as a soloist and as an ensemble player. Tatum is widely credited with completing the transition from the ragtime era to the jazz age begun by his pianistic forerunners, Earl Hines and Fats Waller. Perhaps most famous as a solo pianist reinterpreting such standards as "Sweet Lorraine" and "Tea for Two," Tatum was often lauded for his fleet fingers, light touch, and imaginative harmonies.

JOHN GLENN

ASTRONAUT AND SENATOR

BORN: *July 18, 1921, Cambridge*

After a distinguished career flying combat missions in World War II and the Korean War, John Herschel Glenn, Jr., became a test pilot. He was then chosen as one of the National Aeronautics and Space Administration's (NASA) original *Mercury* astronauts. On February 20, 1962, Glenn made history by becoming the first American to orbit Earth, circling the globe three times in four hours and fifty-five minutes in the *Mercury* capsule dubbed *Friendship 7*. Glenn served in the U.S. Senate, representing Ohio for four consecutive terms, from 1975 to 1999. On October 29, 1998, the seventy-seven-year-old Glenn returned to orbit on an eight-day mission aboard the shuttle *Discovery*. This historic flight made Glenn the oldest human being to travel in space.

CARL BURTON STOKES

POLITICAL LEADER

BORN: *June 21, 1927, Cleveland*
DIED: *April 4, 1996, Cleveland*

Overcoming childhood poverty, Carl B. Stokes earned a law degree and worked as an assistant prosecutor in Cleveland. In 1962 he was elected to Ohio's House of Representatives and was twice reelected. As race riots erupted in Cleveland and cities across the nation, Stokes entered and won the mayoral race in 1967, making him the first African-American mayor of a major U.S. city. The grandson of a slave, Stokes defeated the grandson of President William Howard Taft; Stokes was reelected in 1969. After leaving office in 1971, Stokes worked as an NBC television news commentator; a Cleveland Municipal Court judge; author; and the U.S. ambassador to Seychelles.

NEIL ARMSTRONG
ASTRONAUT

BORN: *August 5, 1930, Wapakoneta*

Apollo 11 liftoff.

After serving as a naval aviator, Neil Alden Armstrong became a civilian test pilot for the National Advisory Committee for Aeronautics (NACA) in 1955 and tested such aircraft as the X-15 rocket plane. Armstrong entered the expanding NASA astronaut program in 1962. He commanded the *Gemini 8* mission, launched on March 16, 1966, during which he and fellow astronaut Dave Scott nearly lost their lives when a malfunctioning thruster caused their orbiting capsule to spin out of control. On July 20, 1969, *Apollo 11* landed on the Moon, and mission commander Armstrong became the first human being to leave his footprints there. Armstrong left NASA in 1971 to become an aeronautical engineering professor at the University of Cincinnati, where he taught until 1981.

HARLAN ELLISON
WRITER

BORN: *May 27, 1934, Painesville*

Harlan Jay Ellison is widely regarded as one of the finest living writers of short stories in the genres of science fiction, fantasy, and horror. In his five-decade career, he has written and edited seventy-three books and has produced more than 1,700 stories, essays, articles, and newspaper columns, as well as numerous teleplays and screenplays. Ellison has received more awards for his body of work than any other living science-fiction writer — the Nebula (from the Science Fiction Writers of America), the Bram Stoker (from the Horror Writers Association), the Edgar Allan Poe (from the Mystery Writers of America), and the Georges Melies fantasy film awards. In 1990 Ellison's essays in defense of freedom of expression garnered him the Silver Pen for Journalism. *The Washington Post* has called Ellison "one of the great living American short story writers."

STEVEN SPIELBERG
FILM DIRECTOR, WRITER, AND PRODUCER

BORN: *December 18, 1947, Cincinnati*

A graduate of California State University in Long Beach, California, Steven Allan Spielberg first grabbed Hollywood's attention with his 1969 short film, *Amblin',* and soon turned his hand to features. *Jaws* (1975) established Spielberg as a leading director, after which he made a series of astonishingly successful films. These films included *Close Encounters of the Third Kind* (1977), *Raiders of the Lost Ark* (1981), *E.T.: The Extraterrestrial* (1982), *The Color Purple* (1985), *Jurassic Park* (1993), and *Schindler's List* (1993). In 1995 Spielberg formed a multimedia company called DreamWorks SKG, with high-profile executives David Geffen and Jeffrey Katzenberg. Spielberg's best work combines a childlike sense of wonder with an expert craftsman's command of the filmmaker's art.

Ohio
History At-A-Glance

c. 1670
The French explorer Rene-Robert Cavelier, Sieur de La Salle, reaches the Ohio region; he may have been the first European man to arrive there.

1750
The Ohio Land Company of Virginia sends Christopher Gist to explore Ohio.

1763
France cedes Ohio to Britain with the Treaty of Paris. Settlers defeat Chief Pontiac's forces.

1772
David Zeisberger founds a Moravian Indian mission at Schoenbrunn and opens the first school west of the Allegheny Mountains in 1773.

1787
Congress establishes the Northwest Territory and sets up the basic government of the region.

1788
The first permanent white settlement in Ohio is established in Marietta.

1799
The Northwest Territory Legislature is established at Cincinnati.

1800
The Division Act divides the Northwest Territory into two regions, with Chillicothe as the capital of the Ohio Territory.

1803
Ohio becomes the seventeenth state to enter the Union, on March 1.

1813
Naval forces led by Commodore Oliver H. Perry overcome the British in the Battle of Lake Erie. After his victory, Perry reports to his commanders, uttering the famous phrase, "We have met the enemy, and they are ours."

1832
The Ohio & Erie Canal opens; the Miami–Erie Canal opens in 1845.

1851
Ohio adopts its present state constitution.

1600   **1700**   **1800**

1492
Christopher Columbus comes to New World.

1607
Capt. John Smith and three ships land on Virginia coast and start first English settlement in New World — Jamestown.

1754–63
French and Indian War.

1773
Boston Tea Party.

1776
Declaration of Independence adopted July 4.

1777
Articles of Confederation adopted by Continental Congress.

1787
U.S. Constitution is written.

1812–14
War of 1812.

United States
History At-A-Glance

The first annual International Sweepstake Race at Cincinnati Motor Speedway. The 300-mile (483-km) race was held on September 4, 1916.

1861
Ohio's state capitol is completed.

1870
Benjamin F. Goodrich begins manufacturing rubber goods in Akron; John D. Rockefeller organizes the Standard Oil Company in Cleveland; the Agricultural and Mechanical College (now Ohio State University) is founded at Columbus.

1914
Ohio passes the Conservancy Act after the 1913 flooding of the Ohio River.

1922
The Miami River Valley flood control project is completed (a similar project in the Muskingum River Valley is completed in 1938).

1955
The Ohio Turnpike opens.

1959
The St. Lawrence Seaway opens, facilitating transportation of goods from Lake Erie to the Atlantic Ocean.

1967
Carl B. Stokes becomes Cleveland's mayor; he is the first African American to lead a major U.S. city.

1969
A fire on the Cuyahoga River gains national attention when *Time* magazine says that the polluted Cuyahoga "oozes rather than flows." The incident inspires massive clean-up efforts.

1970
Four students are killed by National Guard soldiers at Kent State University during an anti-Vietnam War demonstration.

1971
Ohio adopts a personal income tax.

1988
A major oil spill pollutes the Monongahela and Ohio Rivers; decades of radioactive pollution from the nuclear weapons plant at Fernald is discovered, along with an official cover-up of same.

1993
Ohio voters approve $200 million in bonds to improve and expand Ohio's parks and recreation facilities.

1800 **1900** **2000**

1848
Gold discovered in California draws 80,000 prospectors in the 1849 Gold Rush.

1861–65
Civil War.

1869
Transcontinental Railroad completed.

1917–18
U.S. involvement in World War I.

1929
Stock Market Crash ushers in Great Depression.

1941–45
U.S. involvement in World War II.

1950–53
U.S. fights in the Korean War.

1964–73
U.S. involvement in Vietnam War.

2000
George W. Bush wins the closest presidential election in history.

2001
A terrorist attack in which four hijacked airliners crash into New York City's World Trade Center, the Pentagon, and farmland in western Pennsylvania leaves thousands dead or injured.

Festivals and Fun For All

Check web site for exact date and directions.

Buzzard Day, Hinckley

Every March 15 flocks of migrating buzzards (or turkey vultures) return to the town of Hinckley, southwest of Cleveland, as they have every year since 1819. The "Hinckley Roost" draws large groups of enthusiastic bird-watchers.
www.hinckleytwp.org/buzzardday.html

Strawberry Festival, Troy

This celebration of the strawberry comes to downtown Troy each June and includes a parade, entertainment, and craft vendors.
For information, call 937-339-7714.

Heritage Days, Pomeroy

In June visitors to Pomeroy's Meigs County Museum can see displays and demonstrations of the ways of life of Ohio River Valley pioneers.
For information, call 877-634-4726 or 740-992-2239.

Great Lakes Medieval Faire, south of Geneva City

In late June this re-creation of a thirteenth-century fair features musicians, comedians, food, games, and rides.
For information, call 1-888-MEDIEVAL.

Great Mohican Indian Pow-Wow, Loudonville

A celebration to honor Native cultural traditions, including pottery, bead-working, knife-making, silversmithing, food, dance, and storytelling.
For information, call 800-766-2267 or 740-599-6631.

Festival of Flight, Wapakoneta

Held in late July at the Neil Armstrong Air and Space Museum in Wapakoneta, this event honors the astronaut's historic first steps on the Moon. Permanent exhibits include a *Mercury* space capsule and a jet fighter that Armstrong actually test-piloted.
For information, call 800-860-0142 or 419-738-8811.

All-American Soap-Box Derby, Akron

Every July youngsters between the ages of nine and sixteen gather in several Ohio cities to race homemade, motorless "race cars" known as "soap boxes." At stake in the Akron event is the national title.
www.aasbd.org

Pro Football Hall of Fame Festival, Canton

July brings the football faithful together to see the legends of the gridiron as they are honored throughout an entire week with activities such as the Balloon Classic Invitational, Rib Burnoff, Food Fest, fireworks, concerts, a parade, the

Enshrinement Ceremony, and the Hall of Fame Game. For information, call 330-456-8207.

Zoar Harvest Festival, Zoar

Held in early August, this festival commemorates the gathering of the last load of grain from the winter wheat harvest. On hand are more than sixty antique dealers, folk art craftspeople, music from Appalachian to polka, food, and tours of the Ohio Historical Society's museum buildings. For information, call 800-874-4336 or 330-874-4336.

Twins Day Festival, Twinsburg

Each August, twins and their parents from the world over descend on this small town just south of Cleveland for a weekend celebration. www.twinsdays.org

Ohio State Fair, Columbus

Held during the first half of August, the Ohio State Fair is one of the largest annual events in the state. This fair leads the nation in junior competitions. More than seventeen thousand young people compete in agricultural, livestock, fine arts, and craft events at the fair each year. www.ohioexpocenter.com

Ohio Renaissance Festival, Renaissance Park, Harveysburg

From August through October visitors can travel back in time to a 30-acre (23-ha) replica of a sixteenth-century English village. The event includes period entertainment and food. www.renfestival.com

▶ A soap-box derby in Akron, circa 1938.

Ravenna Balloon A-Fair, Ravenna

In mid-September colorful assemblages of hot-air balloons begin flying over Ravenna as the community prepares for the Balloon A-Fair, its celebration of lighter-than-air flight. www/angelfire.com/oh2/balloonafair

Tecumseh (an outdoor play), near Chillicothe

Running from June through September, the historical play *Tecumseh*, a drama about the famous Shawnee chief, is held in an outdoor theater outside of Chillicothe. Performances of this play rank among Ohio's most popular annual attractions. www.tecumsehdrama.com

National Afro-American Museum and Cultural Center, Wilberforce

Dedicated to black history, the museum features a re-creation of a 1950s-era African-American neighborhood. www.ohiohistory.org/places/afroam

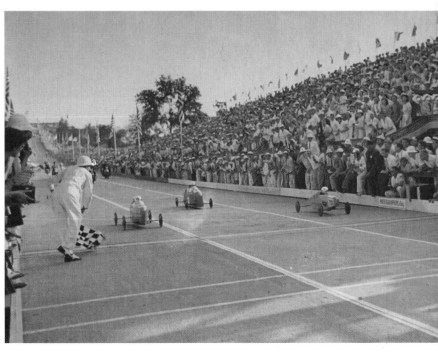

Books

Alderman, Clifford Lindsey. *Annie Oakley and the World of Her Time.* New York: Macmillan, 1979. This Ohioan became famous as a sharpshooter in the wild west.

Brown, Dottie. *Ohio.* Minneapolis: Lerner, 1993. Get to know more about Ohio's history, geography, and environmental issues.

Cwiklik, Robert. *Tecumseh: Shawnee Rebel.* New York: Chelsea House Publishers, 1993. Read about this famous Ohio Shawnee leader.

Erlbach, Arlene. *Kent State.* New York: Children's Press, 1998. A book about an important and tragic event in the anti-war movement of the 1960s and 1970s.

Gaines, Edith M. and Cliff Clay. *Freedom Light: Underground Railroad Stories from Ripley, OH.* Cleveland: New Day Press, 1991. This book about the anti-slavery movement in Ripley, Ohio, is based on eyewitness accounts.

Thompson, Kathleen. *Ohio.* Orlando: Raintree/Steck-Vaughn, 1996. Learn more about Ohio's past from prehistoric times until today.

Web Sites

▶ Official state web site
www.state.oh.us

▶ Ohio tourism site
www.ohiotourism.com
Comprehensive information about Ohio's many festivals, museums, and other attractions.

▶ Ohio State Department
www.oplin.lib.oh.us/products/ohiodefined/message.html
General information about Ohio's history and government.

▶ The American Memory Finder
memory.loc.gov/ammem/collections/finder.html
The Library of Congress has a tremendous collection of primary source material, including downloadable photographs.

▶ Discovery Channel School
school.discovery.com/homeworkhelp/worldbook/atozgeography/
This Discovery Channel site contains abundant geographical resources as well as links to other educational sites.

Note: Page numbers in *italics* refer to illustrations or photographs.